Satin Coated
(Coat is not waterproof)

Albino

Banded

To Sara

With thanks to John Barker, B. Vet. Med., M.R.C.V.S.

First published 1995 by
Walker Books Ltd, 87 Vauxhall Walk
London SE11 5HJ

2 4 6 8 10 9 7 5 3 1

This book has been typeset in Monotype Garamond.

Printed in Belgium

British Library Cataloguing in Publication Data
A catalogue record for this book is
available from the British Library.

ISBN 0-7445-3112-8

How to Look After Your
HAMSTER

Colin and Jacqui Hawkins

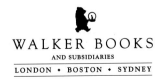

WALKER BOOKS
AND SUBSIDIARIES
LONDON • BOSTON • SYDNEY

Hamster Facts

Did you know "hamster" comes from the German word "*hamstern*" meaning hoarder? This is because hamsters store food in pouches in their cheeks.

There are many varieties of hamster, and they come in different colours, coat-types and sizes.

Golden hamsters are the most popular type. They are all descended from a single female and her family found in Syria in 1930. Because they are desert animals, hamsters sleep during the day (when it is hot) and wake up in the evening.

The Common or European hamster can be very aggressive and may spit when angry.

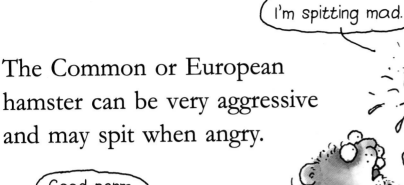

The Rex Coated hamster has curly fur and even curly whiskers.

The Albino hamster is completely white with pink eyes.

Most hamsters will fight when they are put together. Only the dwarf Russian hamster prefers company.

How to Choose a Hamster

Hamsters live for about two years, so choose a young one aged between five and eight weeks. Both males and females make good pets, but make sure that a female has always lived in an all-female cage – otherwise she might be expecting babies!

What to look for

Clear, bright eyes

Clean, dribble-free mouth

Clean, undamaged teeth

Active behaviour

Glossy, well-groomed coat

Ears that are furry inside (this means it is young)

Am I looking good or am I looking good?

Round, plump body

Strong, well-formed feet

Do not choose…

a timid hamster that cowers in the corner of the cage.

a hamster with a runny nose.

a nervous or a panic-stricken hamster.

a hamster that looks dirty or has sores or bald patches, or dampness under the tail.

Bringing Your Hamster Home

A hamster makes a good pet, but before you buy one make sure you have time to feed him, play with him and keep him clean. Bring your hamster home in a comfortable, well-ventilated box.

Once you have put your pet in his new home, leave him to settle down for a few hours. Hamsters are very shy, so make friends gently.

Never poke at the cage with a stick or pencil. This will make the hamster nervous.

A Hamster Home

Cages come in all shapes and sizes. Hamsters are very active and need space to run and climb, so choose a cage with plenty of room for exercise.

Circular, stacking cages are good. They don't take up much room and have several floors for the hamster to explore.

Put absorbent litter such as peat or sawdust on the floor of the cage.

Put the cage in a place that is always warm, but not in direct sunlight…

and well away from draughts.

Make sure there is a nesting box.

Chez Hamster

Hamsters love to burrow, so fill the box with lots of bedding material, such as hay or white shredded paper.

Your hamster needs plenty of fresh water every day. Attach a drip-fed water bottle to the side of the cage.

Every home should have one of these.

Put food in a heavy dish your hamster can't tip over.

Nnnnaa...

Yuk! I hate plastic.

Never use a plastic bowl. Your hamster will gnaw it and plastic splinters may pierce his pouches.

Keeping Your Hamster Happy

997, 998, 999 ...

Hamsters become bored
and restless if they don't
get plenty of exercise.
They can run for miles
on a wheel like this,
but it must have a solid
back and floor, so that
the hamster can't
get trapped in
any open spokes.

This takes years
of practice.

Wooden cotton reels
are safe toys and toilet rolls
can provide plenty of fun.

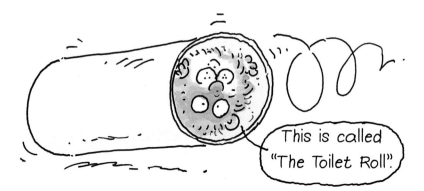

This is called
"The Toilet Roll".

Your hamster will soon learn to enjoy a climbing frame...

and ramps are good for scrambling up and sliding down.

A jamjar is an effective and cheap toy, but make sure it is big enough for your hamster to get in and out easily.

Hamster Food

Hamsters like a varied diet. Mixed seeds, grains and nuts are their basic food and can be bought from the pet shop.

Just off to the pet shop for lunch.

I really love my porridge oats.

They also enjoy a few porridge oats.

An adult hamster needs only about 15 g (½ oz) of food once a day.

I won't need seconds.

I'm always too tired to eat breakfast.

Don't try and feed your hamster in the morning – he will be too sleepy. The best feeding time is in the evening, when he wakes up.

Hamsters love to gnaw, and this stops their teeth growing too long. Let your pet chew on a piece of raw carrot or a dog biscuit.

Hamsters should have some fresh fruit or vegetables every day, and try pieces of hard-boiled egg or flakes of cooked fish occasionally.

Never give your pet oranges, crisps, salted nuts or chocolate. These are not natural foods for hamsters and can make them very ill.

Hamster Hygiene

Help your hamster stay clean and healthy by keeping the cage in good condition.

Once a week...

Put your pet in a safe place and give the whole cage a thorough spring-clean.

Change the litter on the floor of the cage and replace the hay or paper in the nesting box. Always use plain white paper in the box – coloured inks are poisonous.

Your hamster will shred and arrange the material until he's comfortable.

Every day...

Remove any uneaten food before it goes mouldy. In particular, check the hamster's food store for bits of fruit and vegetable that might start to rot.

Thoroughly wash out the feeding bowl and the water bottle. Refill the bottle with fresh water.

Remove droppings. Hamsters can be trained to use a small tray as a toilet. This makes daily cleaning very easy.

Handling Your Hamster

It is important to learn how to handle your hamster properly or he will become bad-tempered and unfriendly.

He may be frightened and try to bite you at first, so be gentle and don't rush. Make sure he is fully awake before you start to make friends.

Hamsters are short-sighted but have a good sense of smell. Let him get to know you by offering him your fingers to sniff.

Once you have made friends you can pick your hamster up. Place your hand gently but firmly over his back and curl your fingers gently under his stomach.

Cup your other hand underneath and scoop him up to make him feel warm and secure.

When you first pick your hamster up make sure you are close to the ground, in case he wriggles free.

Be patient and you will soon have a lovable and friendly pet.

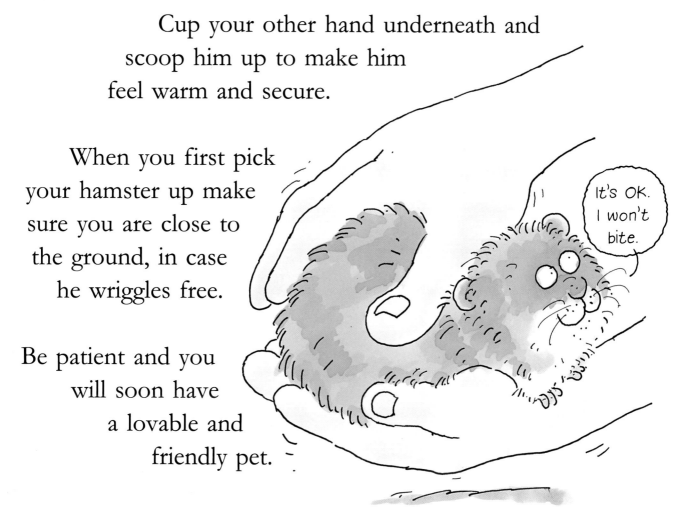

Grooming

Hamsters are very clean animals and will spend a great deal of time washing themselves with their front paws.

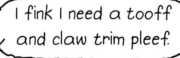

They will bite on hard food like carrots and apples to keep their teeth clean and stop them growing too long.

You should visit the vet if the hamster's teeth or claws get too long.

Very dirty hamsters can be cleaned with a cotton bud dipped in warm water.

Long-haired hamsters need to be lightly brushed each day with a soft toothbrush.

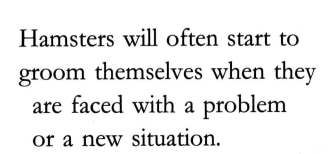

Hamsters will often start to groom themselves when they are faced with a problem or a new situation.

Hamster Health

Hamsters can catch colds or flu from humans, so if you are unwell ask a friend to feed your pet and clean the cage.

Plenty of fruit and moistened vegetables will prevent or cure constipation.

Always remember to wash your hands before and after handling your hamster or cleaning out the cage.

Take your hamster to the vet if…

you think he has diarrhoea or "wet tail". This can be fatal.

his head becomes swollen. It could mean he has an abscess in one of his pouches or that some food has got stuck there.

he has cuts or broken bones from falling or from fighting with another hamster.

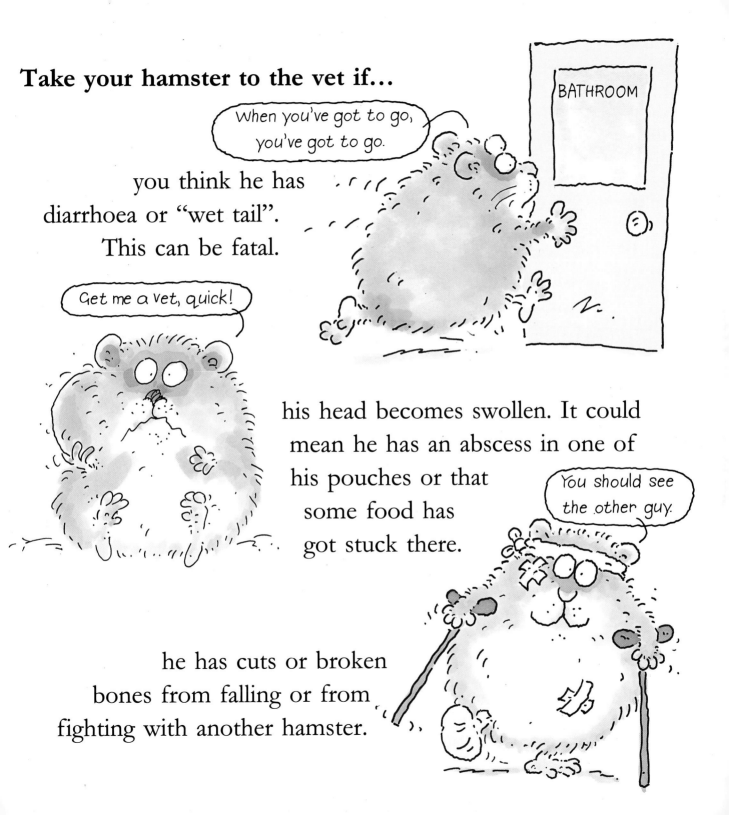

Breeding

As hamsters usually live on their own they will not get pregnant unexpectedly. If you want to breed hamsters think very carefully before you begin. It is quite a difficult business.

Hamsters can start breeding from the time they're eight weeks old. The male and female should be introduced gradually.

The female can get very aggressive if she's put with the male too quickly. Once they have mated they should be separated immediately.

A hamster's pregnancy only lasts sixteen days. She will need plenty of good food and water all through that period.

The hamster mother will not need any help when she has her babies, and you should leave the family alone for a few days afterwards. The babies will be weaned at three weeks old but will start fighting at six weeks, so they will need to be put in separate cages.

Hamsters have large litters of five to seven cubs – make sure you can find them all good homes before you let your pet breed.

Hamster Hints

Never disturb a sleeping hamster. He will panic and may bite.

LET SLEEPING HAMSTERS LIE

KNOCK! KNOCK!

Who's there?

If you want to coax your pet out of the nesting box, tap gently on the side of the cage and tempt him out with his favourite titbit. He will soon learn to come out when you tap.

Hamsters do enjoy a free run out of their cages from time to time, but they are experts at escaping. If your hamster runs away, entice him back with pieces of his favourite food in a jamjar.

What's in here?

Clunk, click every trip.

Hamsters have no idea when they are up high and can injure themselves seriously if they fall. Watch your pet carefully when he's out of the cage and always handle him over a table in case you drop him.

Excuse me, I'm not dead, I'm hibernating.

If the temperature of the cage drops too low your hamster may go into hibernation. If that happens, warm him gently in your hands and let him wake up slowly.

You hamster will have a natural instinct to burrow, so he may enjoy having a tray or bucket of sterilized earth to dig in.

Long-haired Piebald   Golden Syrian   Golden Spotted